BEST OF MARCH MADNESS

MARCH MADNESS WOMEN'S SUPERSTARS

BY CHARLIE BEATTIE

abdobooks.com

Published by Abdo Publishing, a division of ABDO, PO Box 398166, Minneapolis, Minnesota 55439.

Printed in the United States of America, North Mankato, Minnesota.
102025
012026

THIS BOOK CONTAINS RECYCLED MATERIALS

Cover Photo: Jamie Schwaberow/NCAA Photos/Getty Images, Steph Chambers/Getty Images Sport/Getty Images, Ron Jenkins/Getty Images Sport/Getty Images
Interior Photos: Justin Tafoya/NCAA Photos/Getty Images, 4–5; Ben Solomon/NCAA Photos/Getty Images, 7; Andy Lyons/Getty Images Sport/Getty Images, 8, 24, 33, 41; James Drake/Sports Illustrated/Getty Images, 10–11; Peter Read Miller/Sports Illustrated/Getty Images, 13; Gary Landers/AP Images, 15, 45; Otto Greule Jr./Getty Images Sport/Getty Images, 16; Amy Sancetta/AP Images, 19; Elise Amendola/AP Images, 20–21; Todd Warshaw/Allsport/Getty Images Sport/Getty Images, 22; John Dunn/Icon Sport Media/Icon Sportswire/Getty Images, 26; Elsa/Getty Images Sport/Getty Images, 28–29; Greg Nelson/Sports Illustrated/Getty Images, 31; Jamie Schwaberow/NCAA Photos/Getty Images, 34; Sean Rayford/AP Images, 36–37; Ron Schwane/AP Images, 39; Tyler Schank/NCAA Photos/Getty Images, 43; Steve Helber/AP Images, 44; Mike Ehrmann/Getty Images Sport/Getty Images, 45

Editor: Dalton Rains
Series Designer: Ebonee Estrella

Library of Congress Control Number: 2025939195

Publisher's Cataloging-in-Publication Data

Names: Beattie, Charlie, author.
Title: March Madness women's superstars / by Charlie Beattie
Description: Minneapolis, Minnesota: Abdo Publishing, 2026 | Series: Best of March Madness | Includes online resources and index.
Identifiers: ISBN 9781098298197 (lib. bdg.) | ISBN 9798384931997 (ebook)
Subjects: LCSH: Basketball--Juvenile literature. | College sports--Juvenile literature. | Basketball--Tournaments--United States--Juvenile literature. | College sports--United States--History--Juvenile literature. | NCAA Basketball Tournament--Juvenile literature. | March Madness (National Collegiate Athletic Association)--Juvenile literature.
Classification: DDC 796.32363--dc23

TABLE OF CONTENTS

Wilson
24
IOWA
22
TH CAROLINA
41
SEC

CHAPTER ONE

THE SHOWDOWN

Caitlin Clark dribbled slowly up the middle of the court. The star Iowa guard neared the three-point line. Just then, a Hawkeyes teammate moved up and set a screen. That's when Clark kicked into high gear.

Clark's Hawkeyes trailed the undefeated South Carolina Gamecocks 60–59 in their 2023 women's Final Four contest. But when Clark's defender ran into the screen, the Hawkeyes' sharpshooter had all the space she needed. In an instant, Clark pulled up. She rose into the air for a long three-pointer. The ball swished through the hoop. Now Iowa led 62–60. It was exactly the kind of clutch play that had made Clark a national phenomenon all season.

Iowa guard Caitlin Clark (22) made five three-pointers in the 2023 Final Four.

STAR POWER

Over the years, Iowa's women's teams had seen a fair amount of success in the National Collegiate Athletic Association (NCAA) Tournament. However, the Hawkeyes hadn't been a national power for decades. That changed when Clark arrived in the fall of 2020. The 6-foot guard from West Des Moines, Iowa, emerged as one of the sport's all-time great scorers.

In 2023, Clark used her skills on the biggest stage. The junior scored 79 points in Iowa's first three games of the NCAA Tournament. She then put up 41 points, 10 rebounds, and 12 assists in an Elite Eight victory over Louisville. She was the first player to score 40 points in a triple-double performance in the women's tournament.

Next Iowa collided with tournament favorite and defending national champion South Carolina. Clark poured in another 41 points to set a national-semifinal record. With a 77–73 upset victory, the Hawkeyes were headed to their first-ever title game appearance.

Meanwhile, 900 miles (1,400 km) south of Iowa, another budding superstar had surfaced that season. Angel Reese, a physical 6-foot-3 forward from Baltimore, transferred to Louisiana State University (LSU) as a junior in the fall of 2022. Over the course of the regular season, she led the Southeastern Conference (SEC) with 23.0 points and 15.4 rebounds per game.

LSU forward Angel Reese (10) hit 11 of her 19 attempts in the 2023 Final Four.

A fiery player who dubbed herself "The Bayou Barbie," Reese didn't slow down in the NCAA Tournament. Over the first two rounds, she scored 59 points and grabbed 39 rebounds. She also recorded nine blocks and six steals. She then put up two more double-doubles to send LSU to the Final Four.

LSU faced No. 1 seed Virginia Tech in the semifinals. Reese didn't disappoint. She hit 11 of 19 shots, often bullying her way to the basket. She finished with 24 points,

12 rebounds, and three steals. LSU won 79–72, setting the stage for a must-see final against Clark and Iowa.

TUNING IN

More than 19,000 fans packed the American Airlines Center in Dallas for the national title game.

Clark scored 30 points in the 2023 NCAA title game.

Another 12 million tuned in on television. Women's college basketball had been growing in popularity for years, but the sport had never seen anything like this. It was the biggest audience ever for a women's basketball game.

Like she'd done all season, Clark hit shot after shot. However, LSU responded every step of the way. Reese had a low-scoring game with just 15 points, but her teammates picked up the slack. LSU was dominant all over the court. The Tigers hit 51 percent of their shots. They also forced 16 turnovers.

By the game's final minute, LSU had a 16-point lead and was on its way to victory. After an Iowa foul stopped play, Reese lifted her left hand and pointed to where her national championship ring would soon rest. It was a legendary finish to a legendary game. Reese received the Final Four Most Outstanding Player (MOP) Award to go with her championship jewelry. Together, she and Clark had taken the sport to new heights.

THE REMATCH

Caitlin Clark and Angel Reese returned to the tournament in 2024. This time, Iowa and LSU met in the Elite Eight. Reese had a double-double with 17 points and 20 rebounds. Clark got her revenge, though. The Iowa star scored 41 points and lifted the Hawkeyes to a 94–87 win.

CHAPTER TWO

PIONEERING STARS

In 1980, Old Dominion held off Louisiana Tech 68–53 to win a second straight championship. The Monarchs were led by 5-foot, 10-inch point guard Nancy Lieberman. Nicknamed "Lady Magic," Lieberman was a gifted passer. Meanwhile, she racked up record steal totals on defense.

Lieberman was one of many stars of the 1970s who carried women's basketball forward, even with few fans watching. Back then, the NCAA didn't sanction women's basketball. Instead, Lieberman played in the Association for Intercollegiate Athletics for Women (AIAW). In 1981, a feisty freshman point guard named Kim Mulkey helped Louisiana Tech to an AIAW title. With women's basketball growing, the NCAA began its women's tournament the next year. Louisiana Tech

Old Dominion went a combined 72–2 in the team's two championship-winning seasons.

made the switch, and Mulkey once again played a key role as the Lady Techsters won the first NCAA title. After that, the AIAW folded. Mulkey, meanwhile, proved to be only the first of many stars in the NCAA era.

THE WOMEN OF TROY

Cheryl Miller was a well-known star before she ever got to the University of Southern California (USC). She gained national fame by scoring 105 points in a 1982 high school game. However, the fiercely competitive Miller was more than just an elite scorer. The 6-foot-2 forward also used her long arms to swat away shots with ease.

In the first half of the 1983 NCAA championship game, the freshman Miller was outshone by Louisiana Tech's Janice Lawrence. The Trojans struggled to keep up as Lawrence piled up 17 points. Despite 14 points from Miller, "The Women of Troy" trailed 37–26 at halftime.

In the second half, USC coach Linda Sharp had Miller guard Lawrence. Suddenly, the game flipped. Miller shut down Louisiana Tech's star. She also scored 13 points as USC clawed back for a nail-biting 69–67 win. Miller finished the game with 27 points, nine rebounds, four blocks, and four steals. The Trojans' freshman was the undisputed star of women's college basketball. Miller's stellar tournament career was far from over. The next season, she scored the last five points in a

62–57 Final Four win over Louisiana Tech. That put the Trojans into the championship game against Tennessee. Before the game, the fun-loving Miller blasted her boom box in the locker room for a team dance party. She then scored 16 points in the title game. Miller put one of the finishing touches on the win with a steal and layup with 2:19 left. The shot put USC up 61–53. The Trojans went on to win 72–61 as Miller was named the Final Four MOP for a second straight season.

Forward Cheryl Miller recorded seven assists and six rebounds for USC in the 1984 NCAA title game.

OFF THE BENCH

Miller's Trojans hoped to win their third title in 1986. However, coach Jody Conradt's Texas Longhorns stood in their way. Texas was a high-scoring team with a deep bench. In the championship game, the Longhorns' reserves stole the show.

One of Conradt's best bench players was freshman forward Clarissa Davis. The upcoming star averaged 19.8 points per game in Texas's first four 1986 NCAA Tournament games. In the title game, the Longhorns' constant pressure on defense forced Miller into a rare bad game. The USC superstar hit just two shots. Meanwhile, Davis popped off the bench to pour in 24 points. She also added 14 rebounds. Led by Davis's MOP performance, the Texas bench scored 58 points. The Longhorns rolled to a 97–81 win.

Davis soon became a starter. She won the prestigious Naismith Trophy, given to the best college player, twice in her career. Still, upstaging the sport's top player as a freshman remained her finest moment.

COMING HOME

By the late 1980s, Tennessee was one of women's basketball's powerhouses. However, in 1985, a local star got away. Guard Jennifer Azzi grew up in Oak Ridge, Tennessee. Her house was only 20 miles (32 km) from the

Forward Clarissa Davis and the Texas Longhorns celebrate their 1986 NCAA championship.

Lady Volunteers' home arena in Knoxville. Despite that, Stanford coach Tara VanDerveer convinced Azzi to join her in Northern California. At the time, Stanford was a struggling team. But the program's young coach assured Azzi that she would win a national title before graduating.

Azzi was a senior in 1990. Though Stanford had improved, it had yet to win that title. That year, the

Final Four was held at Thompson-Boling Arena, Tennessee's home floor. Everyone had expected the defending-champion Lady Volunteers to be there, but they were upset by Virginia in the Elite Eight. When Stanford reached the Final Four, Azzi was ready for a homecoming.

The 5-foot-9 guard was called "the heartbeat" of the Cardinal. She helped them reach the Final Four

Stanford guard Jennifer Azzi averaged 12.7 points and 6.0 assists per game in 1987–88.

DAWN STALEY

Dawn Staley's Virginia Cavaliers lost to Tennessee 70–67 in overtime of the 1991 title game. But Staley put up 28 points, 11 rebounds, six assists, and three steals. She was so impressive that she was named the Final Four MOP. She was the first player from a losing team to win the award. No player matched that feat in the three decades since Staley's incredible tournament.

with a record of 30–1. Azzi showed it in the semifinals. In a matchup against Virginia, she sparked a first-half run to give Stanford a lead. The Cardinal never trailed again. Azzi led the team to a 75–66 win. Stanford needed more magic from Azzi in the title game against Auburn. Stanford held a slim 48–46 lead early in the second half. Then Azzi dished a pass to a teammate, who made a layup. Soon after, Azzi drained a jump shot. After that, Azzi buried a three. It was one of her four daggers from beyond the arc. Stanford pulled away to win 88–81.

Azzi was named the Final Four MOP. She also received the Wade Trophy for her performance that season. This award goes to the country's top women's player. Azzi capped her dream weekend by welcoming the entire Stanford team to her parents' home in Tennessee. The Cardinal players celebrated the championship with a pizza party.

SWOOPING IN

Texas Tech guard Sheryl Swoopes cut past a screen. Then she pulled up and drilled a three-pointer. It was her third make from beyond the arc in the first half of the 1993 national championship game against Ohio State. Swoopes had 19 points in the half. That was a record for an NCAA Tournament game.

Swoopes had already recorded four 30-point games in the tournament. The Lady Raiders' star guard put on another show against Ohio State. She finished the first half with 23 points. She needed only a few minutes of the second half to reach 29, setting another record for the women's title game.

Using a combination of deep three-pointers, smooth pull-up jumpers, and a few breakaway layups off steals, Swoopes kept scoring. When Ohio State resorted to fouling her in the second half, Swoopes kept the points coming by draining her free throws. Still, with 58 seconds left, Texas Tech was up only 77–73. Then, Swoopes caught a pass at the top of the key. She beat her first defender and split two more Ohio State players at the rim. Swoopes was fouled on the shot, but the ball still dropped through the hoop. The basket gave Swoopes 46 points, topping former University of California, Los Angeles (UCLA) men's star Bill Walton for the most scored in an NCAA title game.

Texas Tech guard Sheryl Swoopes averaged 28.1 points per game in 1992–93.

Swoopes sank her free throw to reach 47 points. That was her final total in the Lady Raiders' 84–82 win. Nancy Lieberman was one of the game's TV announcers. Afterward, the former Old Dominion star said of Swoopes, "People who saw her on national television are going to wake up in the morning and say, 'Wow, she's a great basketball player.'"

CONNECTICUT
50

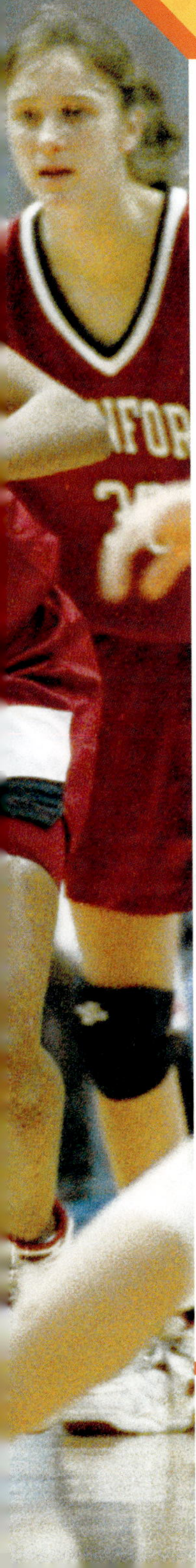

CHAPTER THREE

TOP TEAMS

In the mid-1990s, two women's programs separated themselves from the rest of college basketball. Pat Summitt's Tennessee Lady Volunteers had already won titles in 1987, 1989, and 1991. They faced a new challenger in the 1995 title game. Coach Geno Auriemma's Connecticut (UConn) Huskies were undefeated entering the matchup.

Auriemma's 1995 roster was loaded with talent. Guards Nykesha Sales and Jennifer Rizzotti drained shots from anywhere on the court, and center Kara Wolters provided a physical presence inside. However, the team revolved around Rebecca Lobo. The 6-foot, 4-inch forward averaged 17.1 points per game. She also led the Big East Conference with 3.5 blocks per game.

The Huskies were in trouble in the second half of the championship game. Lobo had picked up three

UConn forward Rebecca Lobo (50) won the Naismith Trophy in 1994–95.

quick fouls and UConn was down by nine. That's when Lobo stepped up and took over the game. Mixing in strong post moves and a pair of long jumpers, she scored eight quick points. UConn rallied to win 70–64 and cap a perfect 35–0 season. Lobo was named Final Four MOP.

THE MEEKS

The 1995 championship game kick-started an intense rivalry between UConn and Tennessee. Each year, they battled to recruit top players. As both schools fought for titles, many of those recruits became tournament legends.

Chamique Holdsclaw averaged 20.4 points per game during her college career at Tennessee.

Lobo graduated after the 1995 season. The next season, a new star emerged for Tennessee. Versatile forward Chamique Holdsclaw often took over games. She showed it as a freshman when the Lady Vols reached the 1996 national championship game. Holdsclaw posted 16 points and 14 rebounds against Georgia as Tennessee snatched its fourth title.

A year later, Holdsclaw put together a run for the ages. In the semifinal and championship games, she piled up a combined 55 points, 12 rebounds, and six assists. Tennessee beat Notre Dame and Old Dominion to repeat as champion.

No women's team had ever won three straight NCAA Tournaments. But with Holdsclaw back, the Lady Vols were favorites in 1997–98. In addition to the veteran forward, Summitt brought in two talented freshmen. Forward Tamika Catchings and guard Semeka Randall both averaged at least 15 points per game. Together, the trio was known as "the Meeks," since all the players had a similar sound in their first names.

The team was at its best in the NCAA Tournament. In a close Elite Eight game with North Carolina, the Meeks combined for 60 points, lifting Tennessee to a 76–70 win. Holdsclaw followed that up with a double-double in the Final Four. Randall added 22 points. The Lady Vols routed Arkansas 86–58.

Holdsclaw added another legendary performance in the title game. The junior outscored Louisiana Tech by herself with 16 points as the Lady Vols took a 36–15 lead. In the end, Catchings led the Lady Vols with 27 points, while Holdsclaw finished with 25 in the 93–75 win. For the second year in a row, Holdsclaw was the Final Four MOP.

A LEGENDARY BACKCOURT

UConn guard Sue Bird had already won a championship as a sophomore in 2000. As a senior in 2001–02, Bird led the undefeated Huskies on a charge for another one. In the Elite Eight, the Naismith Award winner scored a career-high 26 points. She added 11 assists. Many of

LUCK OF THE IRISH

In 2001, Notre Dame put a brief pause on the dominance of UConn and Tennessee. Ruth Riley, a 6-foot-5 center, scored 18 points in a 90–75 Final Four win over UConn. She then had 28 points, 13 rebounds, and seven blocks in the title game against Purdue. Riley hit two free throws with six seconds left to seal a 68–66 win.

UConn guard Diana Taurasi averaged 15.0 points and 4.5 assists per game in college.

her passes went to Diana Taurasi. The sweet-shooting sophomore guard scored 22 points of her own.

The Huskies then blew out Tennessee 79–56 in the Final Four before knocking off Oklahoma 82–70 to claim another championship. Bird ended her college career on top. Meanwhile, Taurasi was just getting started.

Taurasi took over from the start of the 2003 NCAA Tournament. She recorded more than 20 points in each of UConn's first four games. In a Final Four matchup against Texas, she lifted the Huskies to a comeback win. Among her 26 points was a clutch three-pointer to put the Huskies up for good with 2:07 left in the game. In another clutch moment, Taurasi came up with a steal on Texas's final possession. That sealed a 71–69 victory for UConn. The junior capped off a stellar tournament in the title game against Tennessee, posting a game-high 28 points.

The Huskies still had Taurasi in the 2004 tournament. She led the team in scoring in all six games. She posted 17 points in a title game rematch against Tennessee as the Huskies clinched a third straight title.

BATTLING THROUGH

Although Tennessee had a few disappointing seasons in the early 2000s, the Lady Vols couldn't be held back for long. Forward Candace Parker made her first mark on the NCAA Tournament in 2006. That year, she became the first woman to dunk in a tournament game. The Lady Vols fell in the Elite Eight, but Parker was just getting started.

In 2007, the 6-foot, 4-inch sophomore muscled Tennessee through the tournament. The Lady Vols faced Rutgers in the championship game. Despite constant triple-teams, Parker managed 17 points in a 59–46 win.

Tennessee's chance to repeat seemed to take a hit in the 2008 Elite Eight. Parker separated her left shoulder midway through the matchup against Texas A&M. But she

Tennessee forward Candace Parker (3) led the SEC in scoring and blocks in both 2006–07 and 2007–08.

battled through the injury to score a game-high 26 points. In the semifinal and title games, Parker recorded a combined 30 points and 24 rebounds. After Tennessee beat Stanford 64–48 in the final, Parker was named the Final Four MOP for the second straight year.

UConn

CHAPTER FOUR

UNSTOPPABLE PERFORMANCES

Geno Auriemma was often tough on Tina Charles. The UConn coach wanted to push his star center to her full potential. He believed Charles could be the best player in the world. In the 2009 NCAA Tournament, Charles played like it.

Charles racked up three double-doubles leading up to the championship game against Louisville. With the title on the line, the 6-foot-4 junior was unstoppable. She outmuscled any defender who dared enter the lane. After the game, Louisville coach Jeff Walz admitted that his players were intimidated by Charles.

Charles finished the game with 25 points and 19 rebounds. The Huskies rolled to a 76–54 win and finished the season a perfect 39–0. Charles won

UConn center Tina Charles averaged 18.3 points and 12.2 rebounds per game in the 2009 NCAA Tournament.

the Final Four MOP, but even that wasn't enough for Auriemma. The coach said that he couldn't wait to see what Charles could do the next season.

Charles led UConn back to the title game in 2010. At halftime, the Huskies trailed Stanford 20–12. Auriemma called out his entire team during the break. This time, it was junior forward Maya Moore who answered the call. The sharpshooter had been UConn's main weapon throughout the tournament. Moore had scored at least 19 points in each game. That included 34 in a 70–50 Final Four victory over Baylor.

Moore had scored only five points in the first half of the title game. The second half was different. Moore either scored or dished out an assist on each basket in an eight-point run. Then Charles kicked out a pass to Moore beyond the arc. The forward drilled a three-pointer to put UConn up 23–22. Moore finished with 18 points in the second half and 23 overall. A 53–47 win capped off another undefeated season for the Huskies.

BRITTNEY'S BLOCK PARTY

Baylor freshman Brittney Griner struggled against UConn in the 2010 Final Four. The 6-foot-8 center scored only 13 points. A year later, she had another poor performance in the Elite Eight. In a 58–46 loss to Texas A&M, Griner hit only six of 18 shots from the field.

Griner finally put it all together as a junior. Even when the center struggled on offense, she always delivered on defense. Griner's long reach made her a shot-blocking machine. The Lady Bears entered the 2012 tournament 34–0. Through the tournament's first three games, Griner scored 74 points, pulled in in 22 rebounds, and blocked an incredible 15 shots.

Baylor center Brittney Griner (42) swatted down an NCAA-record 748 career blocks.

However, she saved her best performance for Tennessee. In an Elite Eight matchup, Griner nearly recorded a triple-double, adding nine blocks to her 23 points and 15 rebounds.

After beating Stanford in the Final Four, Baylor's perfect record was on the line against Notre Dame in the title game. Once again, Griner was unstoppable. She swatted away five shots. Unable to attack the rim, Notre Dame shot just 22-of-62 from the floor.

The Fighting Irish struggled to find answers on defense too. Griner racked up 26 points. The Lady Bears rolled to their first national title with an 80–61 win. After the game, Notre Dame coach Muffet McGraw called Griner "one of a kind."

STEWIE

Breanna Stewart arrived at UConn in 2012. The 18-year-old forward sometimes got lost in the flow of the play. Stewart was 6-foot-4, gangly, and sometimes looked awkward on the court.

Stewart put in extra work during the season. By the time the Huskies reached the national title game, she was an impact player. Facing Louisville, Stewart capped a stellar tournament with 23 points, nine rebounds, three assists, three steals, and three blocks. She was named the Final Four MOP as UConn won 93–60.

In her incredible career, Stewart played in 22 NCAA Tournament games. She scored at least 10 points in 20 of them. And she almost always piled up rebounds, assists, steals, and blocks to go with her scoring. By the time she was a senior in 2016, Stewart was already the most decorated NCAA Tournament player ever. Her Huskies

UConn's Breanna Stewart, *left*, averaged 19 points and 10.3 rebounds per game over four NCAA title game appearances.

DO-IT-ALL DANIELLE

Texas A&M's Danielle Adams put together an all-around performance in the 2011 NCAA championship game against Notre Dame. She broke a late 66–66 tie with a put-back bucket. Up 70–68 moments later, the triple-teamed Adams fed teammate Tyra White. White then hit a game-clinching three-pointer. The Aggies won 76–60. Adams was named the Final Four MOP after scoring 30 points in the title game. That was the most since Sheryl Swoopes scored 47 points in 1993.

had won three titles, and she was the Final Four MOP each time.

Stewart somehow managed to reach another level in her final season. She opened the 2016 tournament with an 18-point, eight-steal performance against Robert Morris University. Stewart followed that up with three straight double-doubles. She had a combined 64 points, 43 rebounds, and 13 blocks.

The Huskies faced Syracuse in the title game. Stewart capped her college career with another signature performance. She had 24 points and 10 rebounds. And her slick passing skills helped UConn destroy the Orange's full-court press. Stewart added six assists as the Huskies won 82–51.

Danielle Adams (23) averaged 20.2 points and 8.3 rebounds per game for Texas A&M in the 2011 NCAA Tournament.

22
ARIZONA STATE
11

CHAPTER FIVE

MODERN STARS

South Carolina and Arizona State were locked in a tight game late in the second round of the 2017 NCAA Tournament. Sun Devils forward Sophie Brunner tried to go up for a close-range shot against Gamecocks star A'ja Wilson. The 6-foot, 5-inch Wilson extended a long arm and smothered the shot.

Brunner collected the loose ball along the baseline. She took two strong dribbles to the middle of the lane and tried a fadeaway jumper. Wilson reached up with both hands and hammered down yet another shot. Later, Wilson made a clutch basket with 47 seconds left. It helped lock down a win, as South Carolina escaped Arizona State 71–68.

That was just a taste of Wilson's impact on South Carolina's tournament run. Whether scoring a timely

South Carolina center A'ja Wilson (22) recorded 21 points and 11 rebounds in the second round of the 2017 NCAA Tournament.

bucket or making a big defensive stop, the junior forward delivered in every round.

Wilson made sure the Gamecocks had no more late-game drama in the 2017 tournament. She scored in double figures in each game. Wilson put up a double-double in the Final Four. But she saved her best all-around performance for the title matchup against Mississippi State. In that game, Wilson had 23 points, 10 rebounds, and four blocks. Behind the Final Four MOP, the Gamecocks won 67–55.

BUZZER-BEATERS

With 38 seconds left in overtime of the 2018 Final Four, junior Notre Dame guard Arike Ogunbowale had a chance to seal a win. The Fighting Irish led UConn 89–86, and Ogunbowale was shooting free throws. However, she missed her both attempts at the line. The Huskies then tied the game on a three-pointer.

After calling timeout, Notre Dame coach Muffet McGraw called another play for Ogunbowale. But UConn played tight defense to deny Notre Dame's star the ball. By the time Ogunbowale got the pass, she was 30 feet away from the basket. And she had just eight seconds to score.

The 5-foot-8 guard ditched the play and improvised. She dribbled to the right wing, shook off her defender with a quick crossover dribble, and fired a shot from just inside the three-point arc. It swished through the net with one second left. Notre Dame won the nail-biter 91–89.

Most players dream of hitting a game-winning shot in the NCAA Tournament. Few get a chance to knock down a buzzer-beater in back-to-back games. Early in

Arike Ogunbowale celebrates her game-winning shot to send Notre Dame to the 2018 NCAA title game.

the 2018 title game, Ogunbowale didn't seem likely to get the chance. Notre Dame fell behind Mississippi State 40–25 in the third quarter. The Fighting Irish battled back and tied the game in the final minute. With three seconds left, Notre Dame got a steal. McGraw called timeout to set up another play.

Jackie Young inbounded the ball for the Fighting Irish from the right sideline. Ogunbowale came around a screen and caught Young's pass. She was off-balance, but she still hoisted up a shot. The ball dropped through the net with 0.1 seconds left.

Ogunbowale had struggled throughout the game. She shot just 1-for-10 in the first half and finished the game 6-for-21. But the guard was clutch when it mattered most. Notre Dame won 61–58.

DOUBLING UP

Aliyah Boston entered the 2022 Sweet 16 on a roll. South Carolina's 6-foot-5 forward had tallied 26 straight double-doubles. She got off to another hot start against North Carolina. Boston grabbed the opening tip, split two defenders, and made a layup for a quick 2–0 lead. Two possessions later, the junior powered up close to the basket. She missed her first shot before grabbing the rebound and putting it back in. She got fouled on the second-chance shot to set up a three-point play.

Forward Aliyah Boston (4) averaged 16.8 points and 12.5 rebounds per game for South Carolina in 2021–22.

Those two possessions were just the beginning of Boston's incredible game. She went 8-for-13 from the field and 12-for-13 from the free-throw line. She complemented her 28 points with 22 rebounds. The Gamecocks cruised to a 69–61 victory.

Boston's double-double streak ended in South Carolina's Elite Eight win over Creighton. However, she quickly started a new one in the Final Four. The forward had 23 points and 18 rebounds as the Gamecocks beat Louisville 72–59. She then guided her team to a second national title, recording 11 points and 16 rebounds as

South Carolina handily beat UConn 64-49.

CHLOE JACKSON

Chloe Jackson had already transferred twice when she arrived at Baylor. But she made the most of her single season in Waco, Texas. With five seconds left in the 2019 NCAA championship game, the Lady Bears were tied 80-80 with Notre Dame. Jackson drove down the lane and made a layup to put Baylor in front. The Lady Bears held on to an 82-81 win.

PAIGE BUCKETS

Billed as the Huskies' next big star, point guard Paige Bueckers arrived at UConn in 2020. She battled several injuries during her time at Connecticut, but she still delivered on the court. Bueckers led the Huskies to the Final Four in each of her first three full seasons. However, UConn came up short each time. By the 2025 NCAA Tournament, UConn hadn't won a championship in eight years. That felt like an eternity for the powerhouse program.

Bueckers took advantage of her last chance for a title. The senior scored 34 points in a second-round win over South Dakota State. She followed that up with 40 against Oklahoma as UConn rolled to an 82-59 victory. No Huskies player had ever scored 40 points in an NCAA Tournament game before. Next, Bueckers played

In 2025, Paige Bueckers became the first UConn player to score 30-plus points in three straight NCAA Tournament games.

every minute of an Elite Eight matchup against USC. Her 31 points lifted the Huskies to a 78–64 win.

After UConn routed UCLA 85–51, Bueckers and the Huskies faced South Carolina in the title game. Three years earlier, the Gamecocks had beaten UConn in the championship game. This time, Bueckers got revenge. She scored 17 points as the Huskies cruised to an 82–59 victory. Bueckers finished her legendary college career as a champion.

HONORABLE MENTIONS

LUSIA HARRIS

Harris was one of the most dominant players of the AIAW era. She led Mississippi's Delta State University to three straight titles from 1974 to 1976. She recorded 32 points and 16 rebounds in a 1975 championship game win over Immaculata. A year later, she had 30 points and 18 rebounds in the final as Delta State took down Immaculata again.

ANN MEYERS

The pioneering Meyers became the first female athlete to get a college scholarship when she joined UCLA in 1974. Four years later, she led the Bruins to the 1978 national title.

Charlotte Smith

CHARLOTTE SMITH

Smith was dominant in North Carolina's 1994 NCAA Tournament run. She had at least 15 points in all five games. But she is best remembered for her game-winning three-pointer as time expired to beat Louisiana Tech 60–59 in the title game.

UKARI FIGGS

Figgs, a 5-foot-9 guard, put up a double-double in the 1999 Final Four to lift Purdue to a 77–63 win over Louisiana Tech. In the second half of the title game, the senior scored 18 points as Purdue pulled away from Duke for a 62–45 win.

SWIN CASH

Along with Sue Bird and Diana Taurasi, Swin Cash was the third member of UConn's talented 2002 backcourt. The versatile Cash was the brightest star at that year's Final Four. In two games, she piled up 33 points, 17 rebounds, 10 assists, three steals, and five blocks.

Kalani Brown

KALANI BROWN

Brown was overshadowed by teammate Chloe Jackson's game-winning layup in the 2019 title game. But the 6-foot, 7-inch center was a dominant force during Baylor's title run. She had three double-doubles in the tournament, including 20 points and 13 rebounds in the championship game.

GLOSSARY

conference
A group of schools that join together to create a league for their sports teams.

dominant
Clearly better than the opponent.

double-double
Accumulating 10 or more of two certain statistics in a game.

improvise
Make up something on the spot.

inbound
Make a pass from out of bounds to start a possession.

phenomenon
An interesting or remarkable development.

recruit
To try to convince a high school athlete to join a college team. The athletes themselves are also called recruits.

rivalry
A fierce and ongoing competition between two players or teams.

sanction
To officially manage something.

screen
A legal block made by an offensive player against a defender to open up a teammate for a shot or a pass.

seed
A rank assigned to a player or team in a tournament.

triple-double
Accumulating 10 or more of three certain statistics in a game.

triple-teamed
Guarded by three defenders at the same time.

versatile
Able to perform many different roles or functions.

MORE INFORMATION

BOOKS

Flynn, Brendan. *Girls' Basketball*. Abdo, 2022.

Giedd, Steph. *Basketball Strategies*. Abdo, 2024.

Weiss, Sara. *The Totally Awesome World of Caitlin Clark*. Quarto, 2025.

ONLINE RESOURCES

Booklinks
NONFICTION NETWORK
FREE! ONLINE NONFICTION RESOURCES

To learn more about March Madness women's superstars, please visit **abdobooklinks.com** or scan this QR code. These links are routinely monitored and updated to provide the most current information available.

INDEX

ABOUT THE AUTHOR

Charlie Beattie is a writer, editor, and former sportscaster. Originally from Saint Paul, Minnesota, he now lives in Charleston, South Carolina, with his wife and son.